WHAT WAS THAT?

TIM TURNBULL

Donut Press

Published by Donut Press in July 2004.

Donut Press, 46 Lothair Road North,
London, N4 1EW.
donutchops@yahoo.co.uk

Foreword by Clare Pollard.
Edited by Andy Ching.
Designed and typeset by Liam Relph.

Printed and bound by Aldgate Press Ltd.,
London, E1.

ISBN: 0954198344

Happy hour buddies of Donut Press: Tim Wells,
Roddy Lumsden, Clare Pollard, John Stammers,
Karen Ferguson, Dr. Jonnie Williams, Shiona
& Eddie, The Weather Girls, Swiers Bros., Dana
Captainino, A.B. Jackson, Andy, Lorna & Jamie
Green, Corinne Bonfante, James Ruddell, Short
Fuse, Express Excess, & Benny the bartender.

Foreword

Even for those of us who are fans of Tim Turnbull's earlier work, this is an astonishingly good collection. There is a common perception that well-crafted rhyming poetry is rare these days, except for the "light verse" of poets such as Wendy Cope and Sophie Hannah, but whilst Turnbull may be comic he is by no means "light". There are serious, disturbing, heartbreaking poems in this pocket-book - from the car crash scene of *'Et in Arcadia Ego'* to the staggering '9/11', where the disaster is first heard of in a butcher's shop.

Everywhere in *What was that?* we come across remarkable daring - Laurel and Hardy are juxtaposed with the U.S. Marines at My Lai, whilst in Turnbull's bold response to Larkin, 'Not the Whitsun Weddings', the train fills up with bawdy "Stags" and "Hennies" heading north in the wake of the Potters Bar rail disaster.

From the vicious satire of 'Revolutionary Art' to the darkly humorous love lyric 'Succubus', where love "is two parts terror to one part despair," Turnbull continually surprises. This an authentic and original vision of a world where lasses and *Loaded* rub shoulders with high culture and high tragedy. Plus he rhymes Tony Blair with oily hair. Read on and enjoy.

Clare Pollard.

Acknowledgements

Acknowledgements are made to the editors of *Matter* and *Rising*, where some of these poems first appeared.

Contents

The Toerag Situationists

They robbed our lass's Astra GTi in Middlesborough.
It reappeared next day, bonnet removed by bolt-cropper,
stripped of wheels, seats, inlet manifold and wing mirrors.

The stereo was gone and every one of her cassettes,
except, propped on the dashboard, *Elton John: The Greatest Hits.*
And I read in the news that they'd cleaned a warehouse out;

a hundred and fifty thousand pounds worth of CDs
in a single night, but what absolutely mystified the police
was why they'd sorted through them all and left the Bee Gees.

< 1 >

Landcrab

Alec Issigonis's greatest design, the Austin 1800
www.landcrab.net

Once they ruled the earth, these primitive things,
these crude things seen now only in scrapyards
or tarpaulined in urban front gardens,
never-finished projects waiting to be passed
from optimist to dreamer and then last,
their tyres perished, wiring looms hardened
to brittleness, delivered to the scrapyard
anyway, all cracked lamps and dented wings.

There was a time though when half the country
went to work in one or something like it,
when early morning roads rang to the clash
of pressed steel toolboxes hoisted into their
capacious boots, with bradawls, saws, set squares,
and spirit levels slung in in canvas bags,
the spanners, Whitworth, A/F and metric,
chiming out a pre-dawn cacophony.

< 2 >

At night in country lanes and cul-de-sacs
the springs of football field-wide back seats creaked
as, in a mess of pants and Pretty Polly's,
every second citizen was got;
and Britain's favourite flutter then was not
the Lotto but getting them through MOTs.
Brakes were bodged, sills gobbered up out in the street
by sweating oily men sprawled on their backs.

But now these automotive curate's eggs
won't even feature in nostalgic art.
Loaded blokes don't rate them up near sex,
Jeremy Clarkson can or will not love them,
soccer stars and models are above them
and Jay Kay from Jamiraquoi collects
Ferraris, but, in truth, the better part
of that young man ran down his mother's leg.

< 3 >

My Body is Contemptible

His faith in obsolete technology was touching.
The care with which he tensioned the cable,
adjusted the finely machined rods,
attended to the springs and cork pads
of his eight-leading-shoe front brake, moving.

It's a switch, our lad. His brother said.
It's how you set 'em up. He replied
with the air of a Shaolin adept and polished
the alloy cowl. On the downhill right hander,
past the start-finish, on the second lap

his front wheel locked. His wrist broke
on impact and his kneecap smashed but it was
the Matchless behind that cracked his pelvis
and burst his spleen. Marshals waved
gaily with their red flags, glad to be part

of the action at last. The St. John's crew
creaked into life like Disney vultures, squeezed
him, a pallid daddy-long-legs, from his leather
suit and strapped him in the back of their
ambulance. Linda took the car and we,

< 4 >

once it was confirmed that he could still
swear, got ready for the next race. By the end
of the season he was shuffling around the pits
on crutches, whining about his plates and the pain
and saying, *Perhaps we've underrated Triumph frames.*

< 5 >

In the Prospect of Whitby after the Private View

Two faaz'n years of culchah, Mickey Nails
complains and snorts into his beer. He gazes
balefully off down the greasy Thames
as the last charter boat plods its way upriver.

Water laps around the balcony piles. Astrid says
she *tought zat some of it vas good.* We all
agree the painting of the Black and Tan was nicely made.
Astrid liked the shed of vegetable tools

but Mickey thinks the avant-gardists' aspirations
far outstripped their talent or ability
to just get out of bed. The self-harmer stroke
performance artist's photographs of cuts

looked superficial and did not impress us.
Harry Fink points out that he has raised much
better welts on Shel the crack-whore's arse,
while making S&M home movies,

and, come to think of it, she made a mess of his.
Then he gets maudlin because his artistic
output is currently being perused by the Met
and not with a view to sponsoring the work.

< 6 >

In fact they're sniffing round the Pepys estate
to see if all the girls were really volunteers.
When the free pop ran out we came in here,
flush with cash, for more imported lager,

having done a roaring trade in substance
with the goateed wonders in the old tobacco warehouse
on Wapping Wall. It's laughable:
for all the yuppie dockside lofts, the City rich

barred up behind their electronic gates,
who glide like ghosts, in Silver BMWs
and Mercs, the mile or so to work, the Prospect
still fills up with scum and arty hangers-on,

like us, in just the way it's always done. We leave.
The Bangladeshi kids, out on the cobbled street,
stop their football game to stare at us. They stare
as though we're aliens from space -

well dressed but walking, coked up and talking
too much and too fast and heading upstream
to see what the city has to offer.
Oh yeah, two thousand years of culture.

< 7 >

Angel in a Vest

In the late November mist in Tottenham cemetery
among the crosses and the kitsch Victorian statuary
you catch a glimpse of her. In the half-light
between canted slabs, sheets of dripping ivy
and distorted pollards, she appears to glow off-white
and, as she comes into sight, seems to be clothed
in radiant, if slightly foxed, celestial robes.

You read the memorial verse (sub Patience Strong
interspersed with little bits of Yeats and Tennyson)
and circle, keeping her, at all times, in your view.
Closer to, you see it is a tee shirt she has on
all stained with sweat and beer and flecks of food,
the sleeves rucked over her wings, the neck slung low
and on her breast the black and red Bacardi logo.

And yet she smiles, a little simper of a smile,
gazes down upon her charges with hooded eyes
and, underneath the baggy shirt, dispenses flowers.
Her naff Pre-Raphaelite perm shines,
peppered gold and silver by specks of lichen spores
but the robe is far too long. She's not the seraphim
she seemed, in fact hardly more than a cherubim:

< 8 >

a chubby girl as in Charles Burton Barber's masterpiece
Suspense, without the pup and kitten, and cast in concrete.
You stand and stare until the damp soaks through your shoes
and it's time to leave. You straighten out her sleeves.
The last date on the headstone is nineteen fifty two.
A tear of dried-on bird muck stains her cheek.
Suffer little children. Blessed are the meek.

< 9 >

Archie Rice with everything

The fat comedian's looking rather smug.
He's on a roll. He's just done Tony Blair
and wanking, mobile phones and Class B drugs
in nine minutes flat - and they lapped it up.
He dabs his brow, slicks back his oily hair
and, with a sparkle in his eyes, erupts:

McDonald's checkout kids are all as thick
as shit. Where the fuck do they get the staff?
Pizza-faced, illiterate, robotic
and every one's as ugly as it's rude.
He pauses, leaves a hole for them to laugh
then bawls: *You know they spit in people's food?*

Outside the club, the drizzle's turned to sleet.
The burger joint looks welcoming and warm.
The floors are clean, the kids are pretty neat
and have acquired certain social skills,
it's fair to judge from seeing him perform,
our friend the paunchy comic never will.

< 10 >

He nibbles on a fry and licks his lips
and tries to picture, maybe young Anish
aged fifty five and retired as he slips
into a Merc and guns it to the Med
or one-star Joe who joins the *presque riche*
exploiting his small gifts to get ahead.

Next night, the walk-in-wardrobe cum pissoir
that passes for a Dressing Room in Leeds
is full of smoke. The clown hacks up catarrh
and half his lunch, a martyr to his nerves
and the peptic ulcer stomach acid feeds.
He prays we get the fare that we deserve.

< 11 >

Revolutionary Art

This is the one, then. The first great work of art of the new millennium.
A conceptualist masterpiece as audacious in its scale as in its execution.

Rachel Whiteread will turn puce and spit feathers when she hears of it;
the Chapmanbrothers-Hirst-Ofili-Lucas-Emin Axis have a hissy fit.

It makes that bloke in Hoxton who is shredding all his pants and chairs
and fridge look pretty feeble. And best of all it's made by amateurs -

naïve artists who haven't heard of Goldsmith's or Central St. Martin's,
hirsute enthusiasts who, it's safe to say, will never visit Tate Modern

but who challenge our notions of what art is and force us to question
what it's for. They are worthy heirs to the Dadaist anti-tradition,

bold in their unconventional choice of tools and site and techniques,
daring in their use of rocket launchers, tanks and gelignite. They speak

volumes about faith, truth, culture, death and man's inhumanity to man.
Centuries hence art lovers will gaze in awe on the empty vaults at Bamiyan.

< 12 >

Wogs

In the Ziznivy Pes, some dickhead from the Prague Post
orders my girlfriend to keep an eye on his bag and coat.
Watch 'em your fucking self, you dickhead, she says.
Sorry, doll. He explains, *It's just I thought you were Czech.*

Later on, a huge, pissed-up U.S. Marine strips off his shirt
and tells us how U.S. Marines are the best troops in the world
and offers everybody out - one at a time or all at once.
None of the drinkers (English, Russian, German, French) responds.

That night a pair of Gypsies stop some American guy,
who's alone in Namesti Republiky Metro, and ask the time.
He looks at his watch and wakes up stabbed and robbed.
Next afternoon, the joyful word gets round in Josefov.

While we await the northward creep of 90 million
Mexicans, the stretching of supply lines and the slow erosion,
the steady chipping away, time performs on all empires, it seems
we must content ourselves with futile little gestures such as these.

< 13 >

It Lives!

In one gruesome experiment, it seems,
they, with their habitual disregard for
public safety, took the mind of a pig,

implanted it in the body of a pig,
dressed it up in a cheap suit, furnished it
with a full set of opinions and let it loose.

For over eighteen months they monitored
its every move, kept tabs on its contacts
and administered the stabilising drugs,

as necessary, when it slept. Before long,
though, it became clear that they were not
in control at all. They lost track of it

for days on end. The team of specialists
would arrive at the staked-out café to see
a kitchen door flap, an informant shrug

and hear the bins clatter in the next alley.
It has been spotted holding forth in bars
as far apart as Hemel Hempstead, Poole

< 14 >

in Dorset and Hebden Bridge, sometimes
on the same night. In May they thought
they had it, at a Travelodge off the M6

but when the Mondeo door creaked open,
to the orchestrated crash of cocking guns,
a corpulent rep stepped into the spotlights

and crapped himself. While it is at liberty
no woman, man or child can sleep safely.
They will take no responsibility and despite

all evidence to the contrary, all the horror
and fear they have brought into the world,
have begun to deny that it even exists.

< 15 >

Not the Whitsun Weddings

I was in good time but they were late, the Stags,
    and filtered on,
some hefting rucksacks, some Adidas bags,
in odds and sods. Even after London
had jerked into reverse, while I arranged
and rearranged my things repeatedly
(to guard the double airline seat I'd won),
I saw the coach's demographic change
as they moved on, with cool authority,
whole families who vacated looking stunned.

The Stags, though not discreet and not polite,
    were not quite rude.
You knew you wouldn't want to pick a fight
with them but still they managed to exude
a sort of *bonhomie,* tinged with menace.
They'd just annexed the whole half-carriage,
my seats excepted, when I heard a squawk
which indicated they had found the Hennies
heading north, then, like a failing marriage,
the train eased to a halt at Finsbury Park.

< 16 >

It hung in aching heat, among black bricks,
      the journey stalled
above the bagel shops and ticket office.
In daylight, on the bowling alley wall,
a neon tenpin flickered like a loss
and silence fell along the crowded car.
We didn't know but further up the line
the 12:45 out of King's Cross
had jumped the rails approaching Potter's Bar.
Suspension groaned: the linkage whined

and we moved off again on creaking joints:
      the tannoy coughed
and spoke: we waddled over shifting points,
through baking suburbs listening to the soft,
unworldly Geordie burr announcing that
something untoward but comfortably vague
had sent us shuttling over Hertfordshire.
Soon though, the carriage buzzed with bawdy chat;
the Stags had spread out like a laddish plague
infecting half the coach with noise and beer

< 17 >

and I looked round to find the tables strewn,
        a jubilee
of tinnies, all the luggage racks festooned
with photocopies of the groom-to-be's
bare arse. The Stags slipped into rugby shirts
blazoned with the legend *Kibble's Big One*
and while the best man brandished a camcorder
the bolder souls went up the coach to flirt
with Hens they hoped might easily be conned
by pettifogging princes of disorder.

The Hennies played it dumb-but-sly and soaked
        the flattery up.
They sniggered at the boastful, half-cut blokes
and secretly decided who'd get tupped
that night. Non-combatants looked on aghast
as groom-to-be pulled on a dress and stalked
the corridor in drag, Lord of Misrule,
dispensing grog to people as he passed.
We stopped to take on alcohol at York,
the late-arriving, steel-shod Ship of Fools.

< 18 >

Mobiles bleated here and there - relatives
    concerned about
our health but no one in the coach could give
a damn. The Stags had broke the absinthe out
and everything got cloudy; countryside
passed by, a sort of green and yellow smear.
The train, a moral vacuum, was aswarm
with pheromones which hurtled to collide.
Two satyrs rapped on safety glass and leered
at Durham schoolgirls on the platform

who looked away embarrassed and confused.
    And gathering speed
once more we flew, the air perfumed with booze
and latent sex, past Berwick-upon-Tweed
like some absurd prenuptial carnival
for unions that may or may not last,
till, with a shriek of dissipating power
the party ground into the terminal.
In Edinburgh, where partygoers mass
they staggered off, an utter bloody shower.

< 19 >

The Golden Boys

These are the gilded lads in tweeds and cord,
with Dan Dare hair and lustrous brogues,
who vault into their sports cars, with a wave.
They give a toot and speed away toward
some notional future. They'll misbehave,
of course, but are more lovable than rogue.

They never, after all, forget a birthday; just
to send the present or the card or telephone,
and isn't forgetfulness part of their charm?
It's only when the real girls come, to dust
and chatter, break the spell, disturb the calm,
these evanescent princes are dethroned.

From exile, though, it isn't long before
they're summoned up again, by Bell's, on bright,
Haze-scented afternoons, glimpsed from windows
carrying flowers. They never reach the door
but flutter at the edge of sight. Their shadows
must be exorcised by Seroxat each night.

< 20 >

Succubus

How much stranger love is
than he could imagine. She fills
his answerphone with abuse so shrill
it's barely comprehensible.

She leaps from a neighbour's garden
and drags him squawking into the way
of the W3. The bite marks on his nose
and cheek are visible for days.

The bus shrieks and shudders
to a halt. The police are called.
His house is glazed with hardboard.
Rubbish covers his lawn,

graffiti his walls. Love, it seems,
is two parts terror to one part despair.
You can't shake hands and call it a draw.
You just can't declare

because love follows you home at night.
It's skulking in the shadows there.
It lifts tiles and rattles window frames.
Love electrifies the air.

< 21 >

9/11

The first I hear of it is in the butcher's shop.
Tom and his customer stand there gazing up
at the ghettoblaster hanging from a meathook.
They've flown a bloody plane into a tower block.

I imagine a light aircraft, Cessna, accident.
The old fella leans on his stick, says he went
gladly last time and he'd gladly go again.
I scuff the sawdust, draw on the sticky scent

of fat and blood and buy some steak for tea.
Puzzled, back home, I put the telly on.
Sometimes we walk round staring at our feet,
look up and find we're where we started from.

< 22 >

Et in Arcadia Ego

Two fresh black smears on the grey tarmac;
the road dips and curves toward the mountains.

In the dusk, a constellation of fragments -
amber, white and red - of shattered glass

twinkles every time a vehicle rumbles past.
A black hole of spilt sump oil glistens.

Up the verge, where the willowherb is flattened,
there runs a pair of pale brown, rutted tracks

and headlights, after dark, illuminate
flowers in silver paper, hung with twine

around an oak whose bark's torn to reveal
a sheet of cambium, a yellowing page,

foxed and blank. Resin oozes and in time
will cover the wound; will harden and heal.

< 23 >

What was that?

Through a whitewashed courtyard bleached by inappropriate, nearly
    Mediterranean sun
then stoop into a musty junkshop presided over by the murderer
    Christie and Ma Broon.
The rooms have a whiff of elderly relations visited on summer Sunday
    afternoons
with Mack Sennett shorts on the telly, cold pork for tea and, for afters,
    butterfly buns.

Move into the makeshift shrine, all glass cases stuffed with papers,
    scrapbooks, photographs,
film posters, pairs of bowlers and bow ties and the actual *Sons of the
    Desert* hats
and here's some correspondence with a fan, bedridden since her
    unexplained collapse
but delighted they could find the time, and Stan, sick and old and tired
    in a late on-set snap,

bitter since the studio took the writing off his hands and Ollie looking
    fat, even for him, and used.
Cramp into the makeshift picture-house, a room with a big TV and
    salvaged Wesleyan pews
where Ma loads a cassette and off you go - *Scram, Blockheads,
    Laughing Gravy, One Good Turn*
and, best of all, *Big Business.* Watch the stupid escalating war with
    boggle-eyed James Finlayson

< 24 >

where they take turns to wreck his house as he wrecks their car and the
     crowd troop back and forth
and forth and back and the cop double-takes. Writhe and hoot with
     laughter, shake with mirth
at the pie in the face, a hoof in the rump, a poke in the eye, Sartre in
     Africa, a scissored-off tie,
the flaming thumb, firestorm on the Ruhr, marines with Zippo lighters
     strolling through My Lai,

Oppenheimer quoting the *Bhagavad-Gita,* saying *I am become death;
     destroyer of worlds,* a horse
on a piano that makes you laugh until you gasp for air and, lastly, hear
     the music. It's 'The Cuckoo Waltz'.

< 25 >

Also available from Donut Press

Buffalo Bills
John Stammers

TIM WELLS

IF YOU CAN READ THIS
YOU'RE TOO CLOSE

the switch

jonathan asser

All titles £5 (Inc. P&P)

Donut Press,
46 Lothair Road North,
London, N4 1EW.
donutchops@yahoo.co.uk